MONSTERS

A Magic Lens Hunt for Creatures of Myth, Legend, Fairy Tale, and Fiction

WRITTEN BY

Céline Potard

ILLUSTRATED BY

Sophie Ledesma

What on Earth Books

Fascinating or frightening,
monsters are everywhere:
in forests, caves,
mountains and castles,
in outer space or
the bottom of the ocean,
in stories and fairy tales...
Who are they? What do they look like?
What do they do?
Discover their secrets
in the pages of this book,
then hunt them down with
your magical detector!

Beware, each picture is
full of hidden monsters...

① TROLL

This giant is 32 feet (2 m) tall and very ugly, with his enormous nose and awful, spotty skin. That's not all though, he's dumb as a post and as mean as they come. And his favorite meal? Us!

② KORRIGAN

These small, hairy elves from French stories dance in circles as night falls. They set challenges for anyone who stumbles upon them. If the person passes the test, the korrigans grant them a wish. But fail and the korrigans imprison them underground!

③ KODAMA

In Japan, these small, well-camouflaged phantoms are forest spirits. They live in the branches of ancient trees and cry out in distress when one of them is cut down.

④ BABA YAGA

This evil witch from Eastern European legend moves by flying around in a giant mortar for crushing magical herbs. Her cabin is perched up high on a pair of chicken legs and surrounded by a fence made from human bones.

⑤ THE LESHY

This legendary guardian of the forest has blue skin and moss for hair. The Leshy can change into whatever form he wants. He is known to lead travelers astray and abduct children. But, leave him a gift such as an egg, and he might leave you alone.

⑥ GOLLUM

In *The Hobbit*, this gangly creature keeps watch day and night over his precious ring. He has only six teeth, speaks in strange whistling sounds, and catches fish from ponds with his long, slimy fingers.

① SPHINX

This creature has the body, legs, and tail of a lion, the wings of a bird, and the face of a woman. On the walls of the ancient city of Thebes, she asks riddles of travelers. Those who cannot solve them are devoured.

② CERBERUS

This terrifying hound is Hell's guard dog! With three enormous heads, a mane of snakes, and a dragon's tail, he strikes fear into the dead as well as the living.

③ MINOTAUR

This half-man, half-bull is so dangerous he has to be imprisoned in a maze. Every nine years, people must give him seven girls and seven boys to eat or he will break out and kill them all.

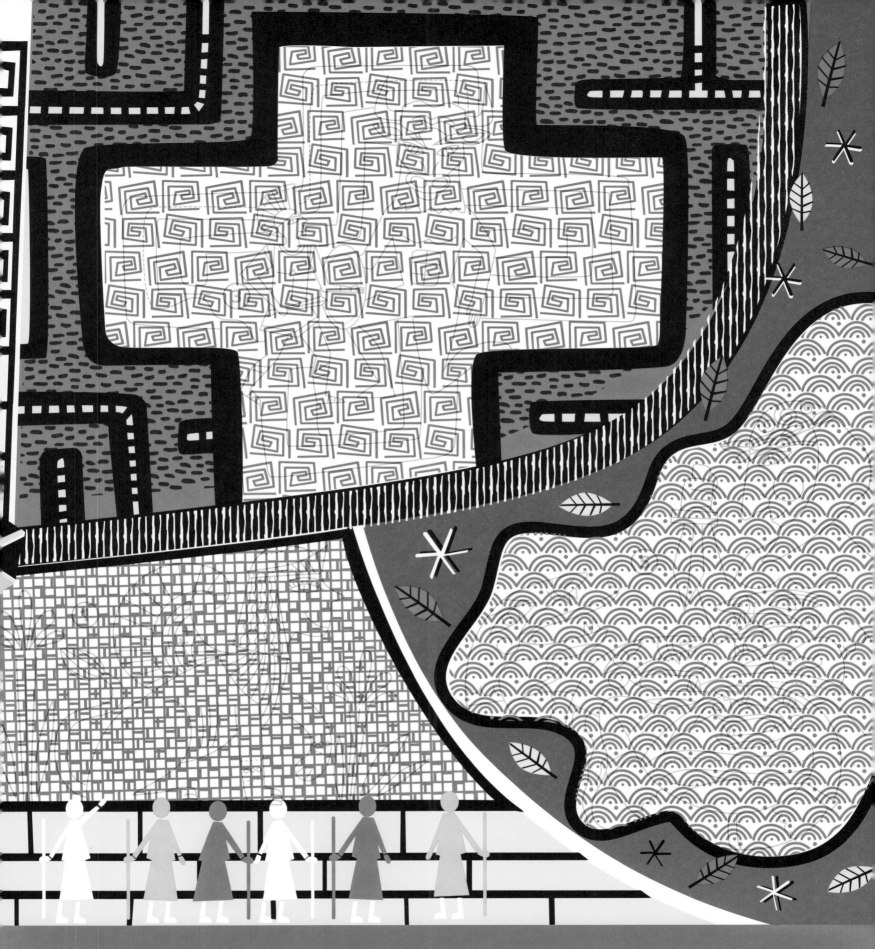

④ CHIRON THE CENTAUR

This immortal monster has the body of a horse and the chest and head of a man! Known for his great wisdom, Chiron teaches numerous heroes, including Achilles and Hercules.

⑤ THE HYDRA OF LERNA

This awful creature lives in Lerna, in Greece. He has dozens of heads and each one grows back as soon as it is cut off. As one of his twelve hero's tasks, Hercules puts an end to this monster with his sword.

⑥ CHIMERA

This strange monster is made up from body parts of a lion, a goat, and a serpent. It terrorizes the local people, breathing fire and eating them and their animals. One day, the hero Bellerophon appears riding the winged horse Pegasus and kills the monster.

BEAST

...tale of "Beauty and the Beast," ...prince is cursed by a fairy who ...d him into a terrible beast. In ...e waits desperately for his love. ...ve can break the spell!

② CASPER THE GHOST

Not all ghosts are scary! In the cartoon *Casper the Friendly Ghost*, Casper was once a little boy. Now a ghost, he dreams of making friends—but anyone who can see him runs away in fear. This unlucky ghost is...

③ VAMPIRE

During the day these legendary monsters sleep in coffins, because they fear the light. At night they leave, cloaked in black, o... transform into bats and fly away. They are... on the hunt for human blood! Run!

④ BLUEBEARD

n this gruesome story, each of Bluebeard's
wives has mysteriously disappeared. At
st, his latest wife discovers that he killed
hem! She escapes before the same thing
an happ... to her.

⑤ DRAGON

The most enormous of all the reptiles,
legendary fire-breathing dragons have
immense wings and sharp claws. They hide
away in castles and mountains, guarding
hoards of treasure. In some stories, brave

⑥ GHOST OF ANNE BOLEYN

Some say that every night Anne Boleyn
roams the Tower of London in a white
gown. In her arms she cradles her own
severed head! Her husband, Henry VIII,
King of England, ordered her beheading

SEA MONSTERS

① THE KRAKEN

This terrifying giant squid attacks unfortunate sailors in Norwegian legends. With its eight powerful tentacles, the kraken drags sailors to the icy depths of the ocean . . . Brrr! So, stay close to the shore!

② MEDUSA

Medusa is one of the Gorgons, daughters of the ancient Greek god of the sea. She has giant teeth and snakes for hair! Those who look into her eyes are instantly turned to stone. Perseus doesn't look at her directly so is able to cut off her head.

③ SEA SERPENT

This long, winding creature hides in cavern under the sea. When it rises to the water' surface to attack boats, it reveals a man of strange spines along its back. And th serpent's favorite snack? Whales!

④ THE FLYING DUTCHMAN

ailors' stories describe this heavily armed host ship. It haunts the seas, traveling wiftly through storms, despite its shredded ails. Even the most daring pirates dread rossing its path!

⑤ MERMAID

These underwater beings are half woman, half fish, with a tail covered in scales and beautiful long hair. In legends and stories, mermaids sing enchanting songs to put sailors under their spell and entice them deep down to the bottom of the ocean.

⑥ LEVIATHAN

Look out . . . this is the biggest sea monster of all! Leviathan is a greedy monster from the Bible: it devours everything in its path and lures victims below the waves by shining a peculiar light.

① GODZILLA

This Japanese movie monster is more than 328 feet (100 m) tall and weighs over 22,000 tons (20,000 tonnes). Godzilla is a mixture of a *Stegosaurus*, a *Tyrannosaurus*, and an *Iguanodon*. He fights other monsters, including Rodan or King Kong!

② BANSHEES

These Irish creatures appear in the form of young girls or old ladies. When they scream, they are foretelling death. Their cries are so piercing that they can even be heard in the middle of a storm!

③ THE JIANGSHI

This Chinese zombie has gray skin and long thin nails. It moves strangely by hopping and sucks out the energy of the living. To destroy it, draw a sacred talisman and stick it to its forehead!

④ MOKELE-MBEMBE

This dragon with a long neck and tiny head lives in the Congo River in Africa. It capsizes canoes with a powerful kick. According to some local people, this dragon is so strong it can change the course of the whole river.

⑤ SELKIE

These magical beings from Scottish legend transform into underwater creatures by putting on the skin of a seal. When they come back onto dry land, they shed the skin and dance naked under the light of the moon.

⑥ THE BUNYIP

The Australian Aborigines call this marshland monster the devil of the swamps. It has a horse's tail, flippers, and tusks like a walrus's. At night, it howls while on the hunt for women—its favorite prey.

① KING KONG

This gigantic movie gorilla is captured on his island and taken to New York, where he climbs to the top of the Empire State Building, carrying in one hand an actress he loves.

② ZOMBIES

In horror movies, these living corpses have eyes that bulge out and skin that hangs off them in rotting tatters. Dressed in torn clothing, they slowly shamble forward, moaning. To make sure they're really dead, aim for their brains!

③ JAWS

This giant shark has razor-sharp teeth and prowls the shores of Amity Island. He traps swimmers and drags them below the waves. In the movie, you can tell he's coming by the scary music and his fin cutting menacingly through the water's surface.

④ EDWARD SCISSORHANDS

This pale young man lives alone in a dark mansion. His creator replaced his fingers with scissors but died before finishing his experiment. He is multi-talented—he uses his scissorhands to trim hedges and cut hair!

⑤ GREMLINS

Feed the tiny, furry creature called a mogwai after midnight, or get it wet, and it will give birth to gremlins! These slimy monsters have huge ears and pointy teeth and can cause mayhem across whole cities!

⑥ THE HEADLESS HORSEMAN

In the movie *Sleepy Hollow* and the Washington Irving story it's based on, this phantom gallops around a quiet village on a black horse. He is looking for his head, which he lost during a war. Watch out, the horseman beheads all who cross his path!

① THE DAHU

This animal from French stories looks like a goat or a deer, but its unusual legs are shorter on one side than the other. These are perfect for walking the steep slopes of mountains. But they have one downside—the dahu can't turn around!

② THE YETI

This gigantic white ape lives alone at the top of the Himalayan mountain range. It is 6½ feet (2 m) tall, has a long skull, and leaves enormous footprints in the snow. Does it really exist? Who knows for sure....

③ THE BEAST OF GÉVAUDAN

According to legend, this monstrous mixture of wolf, hyena, and bear attacked women and children in France 300 years ago. It caused absolute carnage, until it was finally shot by a farmer.

④ ORCS

These goblin foot soldiers have yellow fangs and glaring eyes. In the books of J. R. R. Tolkien, they are commanded by the powerful Morgoth, Lord of the Dark, who controls them with his mind!

⑤ POLYPHEMUS THE CYCLOPS

One of the sons of Poseidon, Ancient Greek god of the sea, this giant has a single eye right in the middle of his head. He loves the taste of human flesh! The hero Odysseus, who he traps in his cave, escapes by poking a tree trunk into his eye, leaving him blind.

⑥ HYPSIGNATHUS

This real-life bat is the largest in Africa. It is also known as the "hammer-headed bat" because of its enormous snout. During the day it sleeps in the treetops, and by night it heads out to feast on the juice of jungle fruits.

OPEN

① QUASIMODO

In Victor Hugo's book *The Hunchback of Notre-Dame*, Quasimodo is abandoned by his cruel parents who can't stand his disfigured body. Raised by a priest, he rings the bells of Notre-Dame Cathedral. He falls in love with Esmeralda, a beautiful gypsy.

② DR. FRANKENSTEIN

This mad scientist creates a monster by collecting together pieces of corpses. Dr. Frankenstein manages to bring the creature to life! Even though his monster is sensitive and intelligent, people flee from it in fear, leaving it to a lonely life.

③ DRACULA

This count with pointy fangs lives in a castle in Romania. He has an intriguing look, with his pale complexion, black hair, and cloak. Count Dracula can change into a wolf or a bat and drinks human blood, which stops him from aging.

④ VOLDEMORT

his powerful wizard from the *Harry Potter* ooks is bald, pale, and has red eyes and two lits in place of a nose. His special talent is peaking parseltongue, the language of nakes. Most call him "He-Who-Must-Not-e-Named."

⑤ THE PHANTOM OF THE OPERA

This unfortunate individual is so ugly that he wears a mask! In Paris, France, he haunts the Palais Garnier Opera House and terrorizes the performers there. The phantom falls in love with a singer he made famous, but she only pretends to love him.

⑥ MR. HYDE

This monstrous man lives in London in Robert Louis Stevenson's book, *Strange Case of Dr. Jekyll and Mr. Hyde*. At night, he commits atrocious crimes. In reality, he is the violent side of Dr. Jekyll, who has two personalities: one good and one evil.

① CTHULHU

This gigantic cosmic entity is found in stories by H. P. Lovecraft and looks like an octopus. Cthulhu is an evil god who sleeps at the bottom of the Pacific Ocean. He is so dangerous that the other space gods have chased him away from his home star.

② MARTIANS

In the film *Mars Attacks!* these little green men with large bulging eyes travel to Earth from Mars. Everyone thinks they come in peace. Really they are here to destroy! Luckily for people on Earth, a certain type of music makes their heads explode.

③ RODAN

This Japanese movie monster is a 328-foot (100-m-) tall mutant dinosaur. Thanks to it immense wings, it can fly at the speed of jet plane. It attacks cities, spreading pani in its wake!

④ GARGOYLE

a French fairy tale, a dragon kills the
eople of Rouen by unleashing torrents
f water from its mouth. But St. Romanus
ves the village by setting the dragon on
re. His head and neck are turned to stone
d used to decorate buildings.

⑤ HARPIES

These three dreadful sisters are monsters
from Greek mythology. They smell awful
and have the bodies of birds and the heads
of women. With their pointed claws, they
snatch the souls of the dead and even the
souls of living children!

⑥ JABBA THE HUTT

This gangster is from the *Star Wars* films and
looks like a giant slug. His passions include
telling lies, stuffing himself with food, and
cheating people. Those who stand in his
way are eaten by the rancor, a monster he
keeps locked away underneath his palace.

① OGRE

In books and legends, ogres are terrible giants who like to feast on human flesh! Ogres have a strong sense of smell, so they can sense humans coming from miles away and turn them into dinner.

② WYVERN

This legendary swamp creature is a flying serpent with wings. On its chest it wears a fantastic ruby. Beware to those who try to steal the gem—the wyvern will make mincemeat out of you!

③ THE SEA WITCH

In the fairy tale of "The Little Mermaid," thi awful witch lives deep in the depths of th ocean. She gives a magic potion to the littl mermaid, transforming her tail into legs s she can live on land with her prince. But i return she steals the mermaid's voice!

④ THE BIG BAD WOLF

n the story of "Little Red Riding Hood,"
his villainous wolf hides out in the deep
ark woods. He has such big ears and such
ig teeth—all the better to eat children
ith! To devour Little Red Riding Hood, he
isguised himself as her grandmother.

⑤ THE GREEDY WITCH

This evil witch lures children into her
gingerbread house with candy in the
story of "Hansel and Gretel." She traps
Hansel in a cage so she can fatten him up
and eat him, but his sister Gretel saves him
just in time.

⑥ THE GIANT

This giant has colossal feet and hands. He is
so strong, he can squeeze a rock like it's a
sponge and carry an entire tree by himself.
But his huge size is no match for a cunning
human in the story of "Brave Little Tailor"!

① WEREWOLF

European legends tell how werewolves sprout hair and turn into half-man, half-wolf creatures under the light of a full moon. Anyone unfortunate enough to be bitten by a werewolf will become one too. Only

② THE BOGEYMAN

In stories from all across the world, this ruthless monster lurks under children's beds and grabs them at night! Remember to check before you sleep and you'll be fine. But if you haven't been careful, he

③ THE DAME BLANCHE

At night, this spirit appears to drivers o the roads, her ghostly figure dressed a in white. But she doesn't want to scar those passing by—she tries to warn ther of imminent danger. Soon afterward, sh